SHOCK ZONE™
DEADLY AND DANGEROUS

DEADLY
High-Risk
JOBS

ELAINE LANDAU

Lerner Publications Company • Minneapolis

For Kassandra Marie Troncoso—a girl with a hearty appetite for trying new things! —EL

Lerner Publications Company
A division of Lerner Publishing Group, Inc.
241 First Avenue North
Minneapolis, MN 55401 U.S.A.

Website address: www.lernerbooks.com

Library of Congress Cataloging-in-Publication Data

Landau, Elaine.
    Deadly high-risk jobs / by Elaine Landau.
        p.   cm. — (Shockzone™—deadly and dangerous)
    Includes index.
    ISBN 978–1–4677–0603–2 (lib. bdg. : alk. paper)
    1. Hazardous occupations—Juvenile literature. I. Title.
HD7262.L28 2013
331.702—dc23   2012012237

Manufactured in the United States of America
1 – MG – 12/31/12

TABLE OF CONTENTS

Ever think about jobs?

After all, almost everyone does some kind of work. Some people wear suits to their jobs. They use computers, sell things, or help others solve problems. Jobs like these are fine, but they aren't for everyone. A smaller group of people choose very different types of work. These workers do some of the dirtiest and most dangerous jobs around. When they leave for work, there is always a chance that they won't be back. Seeing their family and friends again can depend on what happens at work that day.

Do you have the steady hands it takes to disarm an explosive device? Find out more on page 12.

Their jobs include all kinds of crazy, nasty, kick-your-butt tasks. And their work often calls for some very special skills—not to mention tons of guts and daring. A typical day may have these workers disarming ticking bombs or jumping from planes to put out blazing forest fires. After learning about jobs like these, you might want to try one someday. Or you might want to choose anything *but* this type of career! Read on and see what you think.

Jumping from a plane to battle flames is all in a day's work for this brave firefighter.

Alaskan Crab Fisher

Imagine this: It's a bitterly cold day. You're working on a crab boat in the freezing, unforgiving waters between Alaska and Russia. This is no nine-to-five job. You work eighteen- to twenty-hour shifts on this gig.

Today you and some of the other crew members are on the icy deck as hail the size of mothballs begins to fall. The 40-foot (12-meter) waves rock the boat as if it were a bathtub toy. You're at the mercy of the weather and the sea as you help haul up the 800-pound (363-kilogram) crab cages from the bottom of the ocean.

It's hard, dangerous work. You can get caught up in the cage's coil lines. Both fingers and hands have been severed when trapped between the rope and the electric pulley used to bring up the cages.

You're also working at the boat's edge. You can easily fall overboard. You don't want that to happen, since the freezing waters can kill you in an instant.

Drowning is another risk. At times, smaller fishing boats have capsized in monster waves. In these cases, more than one crew member drowned.

capsized = turned upside down

All these things have made some call crab fishing the world's dirtiest and deadliest job. Each year lives are lost in this industry. Yet the pay is good. Crab fishing may just be the worst job with the best pay. Some fishers believe that surviving on an Alaskan crab boat makes them stronger and improves their fishing skills. Still, you can't deny it: Alaskan crab fishing is one crazy, high-risk job.

SMOKE JUMPER

Fire! It's a frightening word. Most people run from fires. But not the people who fight wilderness fires. They parachute out of aircrafts to put out blazing forest fires. They're known as smoke jumpers.

Jumping thousands of feet from a plane is really dangerous. If a smoke jumper's landing is rough or if the parachute fails, he or she can easily break bones or wind up dead. But parachuting into the wilderness is just the beginning. As soon as a smoke jumper's feet touch the ground, he or she starts battling flames.

Putting out forest fires is both risky and grueling. A smoke jumper may fight a blaze for days. What's more, forest fires often swiftly change their path. A lot depends on the weather and the way the wind is blowing. Smoke jumpers who've become trapped by fires have burned to death in a wall of flames.

Smoke jumpers often spend anywhere from fourteen to eighteen hours a day at work. Even after the blaze is under control, they have to stay on the scene. They get down on the ground to feel for any hot spots. They check every inch of the burn area with their bare hands. A hot spot could make the fire start up again.

Leaving the area can be even tougher than getting there. The smoke jumpers have to pack up all their gear and get to the nearest open area where they can be picked up. That can mean walking more than 5 miles (8 kilometers) while carrying 115 pounds (52 kg) of gear.

Axes are one of the tools that smoke jumpers use to fight fires.

YOU GOTTA BE TOUGH!

On the first day of smoke jumper training, you must pass a physical test. You have to be able to do the following:

- Seven chin-ups
- Forty-five sit-ups
- Twenty-five push-ups
- Run 1.5 miles (2.4 kilometers) in fewer than eleven minutes

Talk about intense! Could *you* make the cut?

9

Stunt Performer

Do you like action movies? They offer thrills and chills. You're likely to see car crashes and people leaping off cliffs. Maybe someone on fire will flee an exploding building.

Sometimes the effects for scenes like these are created with computers. But in other cases, real people do death-defying moves to bring these scenes to life. These people are stunt performers.

Stunt work is really dangerous. You have to be highly skilled. Often these performers spend years practicing their craft. The work can be tiring too. Stunt performers put in long days under

Doing stunts means taking real risks. These risks are beyond what most actors will endure. Injuries are common in stunt work. Crash scenes are especially dangerous. Stunt performers have wound up paralyzed after flying off motorcycles while filming crash scenes. Paralysis has also struck stunt car drivers when their car's front end got bashed in during crashes. Such crashes have killed many drivers too.

In spite of the dangers, Hollywood has many stunt performers. Who would do this work? People who crave action, adventure, and risk.

These men perform a stunt on the set of *Sherlock Holmes*.

ARMY BOMB SQUAD EXPERT

What if you had to work with **explosives** every day? That's the reality for the brave folks on the U.S. Army bomb squad. These men and women spend their time disarming IEDs and other dangerous devices.

IEDs = improvised explosive devices. Improvised explosive devices are homemade bombs that enemies often leave on roadsides during wartime.

Working on the U.S. Army bomb squad is a tricky job, to say the least. Sometimes the enemy places a fake IED near a road to fool the bomb squad. The real bomb might be a ways up the road. If the bomb squad misses the real bomb, several bomb squad vehicles could be blown up. Team members could be killed.

Machines such as this one help army bomb squad experts examine bombs.

When a bomb squad is handling a real bomb, the danger can be even greater. They must examine it knowing full well that it could explode at any second. If a bomb explodes, it can easily blow off arms and legs. It can kill whoever is inspecting it, plus anyone who's standing even remotely close to the bomb.

The bomb squad also often helps in raids on buildings where IEDs are being made. Sometimes these go smoothly. But at times, there may be an all-out firefight. These raids have lessened the number of IED attacks. Yet some attacks continue. U.S. Army bomb squad members still risk their lives every day trying to stop them.

This expert wears a special suit to protect him while working with explosives.

Deep-Sea Diver

Most people work on land. But can you picture working under the sea? That's what deep-sea divers do. It's like being in another world. Their work is exciting, but it can also be risky.

Deep-sea divers do many underwater jobs. Often it's hard, dirty work. Many repair bridges and oil rig systems. Can you see yourself beneath the sea with a cutting torch in your hand?

Deep-sea divers also do recovery work. Some are specially trained to recover bodies after boating accidents. Stray fishing lines can ensnare divers when they're pulling up bodies from heavily fished waters. Getting stuck underwater is a problem, since the air in divers' oxygen tanks only lasts so long.

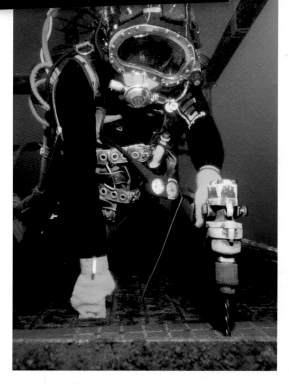

You have to be mentally sharp to be a deep-sea diver. You must know what to do if something goes wrong with your equipment. You can't afford to panic at the sight of a shark either. Frantic movements and splashing attract hungry sharks.

Deep-sea diving can also involve other risks. One of the most common is called the bends. In such cases, a gas called nitrogen builds up in the diver's tissues and bloodstream. This can cause extreme pain in the arm and leg joints; skin rashes and itching; aches in the head, neck, and torso; and weakness on one side of the body. The bends can strike when divers come up too quickly. It can also happen if they dive too deeply or for too long. If left untreated, the bends can kill you.

In spite of the dangers, some people still want to be deep-sea divers. They can't see themselves in an office. They'd much rather spend their workday in an underwater world.

These men use their diving skills to perform a recovery mission.

SWAT TEAM MEMBER

A bank robbery is in progress, and lives are at stake. Four armed robbers are holding a group of hostages inside the bank. You are one of the law enforcement officers called in to rescue the hostages.

The robbers might shoot to kill at any time. You're wearing heavy body armor. Yet you know you're walking into a potentially deadly scene.

What kinds of cops face such high-stakes situations every day? They're called SWAT (Special Weapons and Tactics) team members. SWAT teams are top-notch units in law enforcement. Its members handle risky calls that most police officers haven't been trained for.

The lives of SWAT team members are filled with danger. They can be targeted by terrorists with stockpiles of weapons. Violent crowds can attack them if they're called to riot scenes. Grave injuries and death are par for the course when you're chasing angry people who don't want the cops involved.

SWAT teams are called in to capture dangerous criminals.

SWAT teams receive special training to help them try to stay alive in such scenarios. All team members have to be in peak physical shape. They are required to do push-ups, sit-ups, and weight training.

SWAT team members must also be outstanding marksmen. They spend hours practicing on moving targets. Some on the team receive further special training. They are trained to be snipers and explosives experts.

Being in high-risk situations is just part of a SWAT team member's job. Some people see them as heroes and want to be on a SWAT team someday. Others feel the job is too dangerous. Yet facing danger is what being a SWAT team member is all about.

snipers =
expert marksmen
who stay hidden
from view

This sniper uses the sight on his rifle to find his target.

BOUNTY HUNTER

"Wimps need not apply." This just might be the perfect slogan for the job of bounty hunter. Bounty hunters are paid to bring in fugitives. Those are people who are wanted by the law but failed to appear in court for their trials.

Catching fugitives can be extremely hard. Usually these people are on the run and don't want to be found. Many are armed and dangerous. Bounty hunters have often had to dodge bullets. And even when the wanted person is unarmed, there may still be trouble. Some fugitives have fought bounty hunters in bloody hand-to-hand combat. Bounty hunters never know what they'll face on a job.

Bounty hunters need to be in good physical shape. When chasing a person, they may have to crawl across a narrow attic or scale a rooftop. It's not uncommon for bounty hunters to have to kick down doors as well.

The bounty hunter's most important tools are brains and cunning. Bounty hunters must outsmart the criminal. Their job is easier if they can surprise the wanted person. That's why bounty hunters often show up in the middle of the night. At times, they also pose as delivery people to get into the wanted person's home.

No one ever said that bounty hunting is easy. Yet many who do it say they love their work. They live for the excitement of the chase. They also enjoy bringing criminals to justice.

Bounty hunting is a dangerous profession—it's considered even riskier than alligator wrestling!

Race Car Driver

Few things beat the thrill of car racing. Lots of people love to watch car races. But some people take their love for racing a step further. They're not happy unless they're behind the wheel of a race car!

Race car driving is a thrilling job. But is it safe? No way! On some tracks, you have about thirty-four cars going at high speeds. There are lots of turns and curves. At times, cars are just inches from one another. A car can go airborne or flip upside down and skid across the track. A driver can slam into the wall headfirst. In car pileups, some cars have burst into flames.

Crashes are the biggest risk to race car drivers. Even if they live, some drivers who've crashed have been left brain damaged or lost arms and legs. Many have been paralyzed or forced to live with terrible pain.

There are other health risks as well. Race car drivers and their crews inhale all sorts of toxic fumes. These come from gasoline, burning rubber, and secondhand cigarette smoke. Such fumes can lead to cancers and other health problems.

Hearing loss is still another risk. The noise at a race car track can be crazy loud—even louder than a rock concert. Most drivers and their crews wear earplugs. But some race car drivers still have hearing loss.

Yet is race car driving still popular? You bet! Drivers dream of winning. The prize money for winning big races can be in the millions. For those who race, the reward is worth the risk.

Car wrecks happen a lot on high-speed racetracks.

NAVY SEAL

You're on a **mission.** You have to ambush a unit of terrorists and bring them in. Before leaving, you must destroy their stock of weapons. You're counting on surprising the enemy. But it won't be easy.

> **ambush** = a surprise attack made from a hidden position

This is a high-risk operation. These terrorists are shrewd fighters. They wouldn't hesitate to shoot you point-blank. They could also attack you with the weapons they have stockpiled.

Even if you defeat the enemy and get to their weapons, plenty still could go wrong. If they have bombs in their arsenal—and they probably do—those bombs could explode. Bombs could blow your arms and legs off. Or they might kill you on the spot.

What job do you have that has you facing such dire circumstances? You're a Navy SEAL. The good news is that you're among the toughest, best-trained fighters in the world.

Navy SEALS are a special operations force in the U.S. Navy. The term *SEAL* stands for Sea, Air, and Land. SEALs are trained to work in all three of these areas. They go on some of the most dangerous missions. They get in and out quickly. Navy SEALS are trained to do the unexpected, and they do it amazingly well.

Not everyone can be a SEAL. For starters, you must be an active-duty member of the U.S. Navy. Just to apply, you have to be able to do forty-two push-ups in under two minutes. You also must be able to run long distances wearing heavy armor.

Navy SEALs know their lives are on the line. But they don't let fear get in the way. Many people long to be SEALs. But few make the cut. Those who do willingly risk their lives for their country.

These Navy SEALs approach the land from the ocean carrying up to 50 pounds (23 kg) of gear.

ASTRONAUT

Have you dreamed of being an astronaut? Many people do. But being on a space crew isn't all glory. It's one of the riskiest jobs around. Astronauts put their lives on the line every time they go into space. This job isn't for the faint of heart.

What can go wrong when you're traveling into space? For starters, you're aboard a highly technical vehicle that's hurtling through the atmosphere at 17,500 miles (28,000 km) per hour. Its mechanics are complex, and the slightest glitch could result in disaster. Explosions, fires on board the spacecraft, and engine failures are all things that can go wrong. Take the disintegration of the spacecraft *Challenger* in 1986. A leak in one of the vehicle's solid rocket boosters caused a fuel tank to catch fire, which made the shuttle explode in midair. All seven crew members died. Such risks are ones astronauts must accept if they want to go to space.

Space shuttle *Atlantis* blasts off.

Other risks are more gradual, but they're no less dangerous. For example, cancer is a risk of space travel. Why? There's radiation in space. This powerful form of energy has been linked to cancer. Trips into space—especially trips of six months or more—mean plenty of exposure to radiation.

Spaceflights can also harm the crews' bones. In a low-gravity place like space, bones weaken. That's because bones get stronger when small amounts of stress are put on them. Gravity puts stress on bones because bones have to work against gravity to support the body. When there's little gravity, bones no longer have this stress. Weaker bones means a greater risk for fractures.

In spite of all the dangers, many young people still want to be astronauts. Is it worth the risks? They think so. They'll face any danger to explore this exciting frontier.

Space suits protect astronauts in case of emergency.

Rodeo Bull Rider

Think football, ice hockey, or boxing are dangerous?
Forget about it. Those pro sports don't compare with the risks
rodeo bull riders face. In bull riding, the rider has to stay on the
bull for eight seconds. But there's a problem. The bulls don't
want to be ridden.

The bulls weigh from 1,000 to 2,000 pounds (454 to 907 kg). That's
more than fifteen times the weight of most riders. A bull that size
can throw a rider about 20 feet (6 m) into the air.

But that's not the worst that can happen. After the rider lands, the
bull may charge the fallen rider at full speed. The horns, hoofs, and
hard heads of these animals can do a lot of damage. Bulls have
stomped on riders, smashing their skulls. Often these riders have
been left brain damaged. Some riders have hurt their necks and

Bulls are confined to small metal pens to contain their wild bucking so the rider can get onto the bull's back.

backs and been paralyzed. Others have had damaged spleens, livers, and other organs. Still other riders have died.

Bull riding is one of the most popular rodeo events. The crowds love it because of the danger. Many bull riders have become rodeo stars. They try not to think about the risks. The pay is good, and they enjoy the excitement too. Some even have a special motto: if you've got the skill, you can't beat the thrill.

Once a rider is thrown, he must quickly get on his feet to get out of the range of the bull.

WAR ZONE REPORTER

Do you have a nose for news? Maybe you like being where the action is. If so, someday you might want to be a news reporter in a war zone. But don't be too quick to apply for this job. Reporting from combat areas can be extremely dangerous.

Sometimes war zone reporters are sent to places where no one is safe. Over the years, some have been injured, taken hostage, and tortured. An explosive does not know the difference between a soldier and a reporter. One reporter lost his right hand during the Iraq war (2003–2011). It happened when a grenade was tossed into a patrol car he was riding in.

Snipers are still another danger. At times, they'll shoot into a crowd to cause a panic. They don't care whom they hit. Sometimes they'll hit reporters.

Other times, reporters sent to cover a conflict become the enemy's target. This may have happened in February 2012 during a violent uprising in Syria. An American reporter and a French photographer were killed there. Some think the Syrian government may have given orders to target newspeople. That way, the world would not hear about what was really going on in the country.

Reporting in war zones can also be very exciting. You see combat action firsthand. But you've got to be brave. You can't head back to your hotel when the bullets start flying. War zone reporters are usually well paid. You just hope you'll stay alive and well enough to cash your paycheck.

Journalist Marie Colvin stands in Tahrir Square in Cairo, Egypt. She was killed in Syria in 2012. She lost her eye during a dangerous reporting trip to Sri Lanka in 2001.

BLS Career Information
http://www.bls.gov/k12
This site has all kinds of info on jobs for kids and teens. Just click on what you like—from building and fixing things to sports or computers—and this site will show you jobs that match your interests.

Gross, Miriam. *All about Astronauts*. New York: PowerKids Press, 2009.
Check out this fun, simple read to learn all about the history of the space program. There's also lots of info on the training and activities of astronauts today.

Hamilton, John. *Navy SEALs*. Edina, MN: Abdo, 2012.
Interested in being a Navy SEAL? This book will fill you in on the history and mission of this special operations force. You'll also learn about their stealth and guerrilla warfare tactics.

Loveless, Antony. *Bodyguards*. New York: Crabtree, 2010.
Is being a bodyguard dangerous? You bet! This book shows how bodyguards regularly put their safety on the line to protect others.

Loveless, Antony. *Bomb and Mine Disposal Officers*. New York: Crabtree, 2010.
Working with explosives is really dangerous, but some people do it every day. This book will show you how bomb disposal experts use their skills to save lives.

Mallory, Kenneth. *Adventure Beneath the Sea: Seven Days in an Underwater Laboratory*. Honesdale, PA: Boyds Mills Press, 2010.
Ever wonder what it would be like to go beneath the sea? Find out in this interesting book about being in an underwater science station. Be sure to check out the colorful photos of this very wet world.

Smoke Jumpers
http://www.fs.fed.us/fire/people/smokejumpers
Visit this exciting website to learn all about smoke jumping basics. It offers some great info on the people who jump out of airplanes to fight forest fires.

Thomas, Isabel. *Being a Stunt Performer*. Minneapolis: Lerner Publications Company, 2013.
Want to read more about being a stunt performer? Then this book is right up your alley.

Tieck, Sarah. *Smoke Jumpers*. Edina, MN: Abdo, 2012.
Here's a close-up, action-packed look at what smoke jumpers do. You'll also learn about the history of smoke jumping and the special gear and tools smoke jumpers use.

LERNER
SOURCE
Expand learning beyond the printed book. Download free, complementary educational resources for this book from our website, www.lerneresource.com.

PHOTO ACKNOWLEDGMENTS

The images in this book are used with the permission of: U.S. Army Photo by Jim Bryant/Northwest Guardian, p. 4; © Fairbanks Daily News-Miner/ZUMA Press, p. 5; © Accent Alaska.com/Alamy, p. 6; © Erik Hill/Anchorage Daily News/Getty Images, p. 7; © Darin Oswald/Idaho Statesman/McClatchy Tribune/Getty Images, p. 8; © Tyler Stableford/Stone/Getty Images, p. 9 (top); © Chris Butler/ZUMA Press, p. 9 (bottom left); Photo by Dylan Reeves, California Smokejumpers, USDA Forest Service, p. 9 (bottom right); AP Photo/The York Dispatch, Jason Plotkin, p. 10; Courtesy Everett Collection, p. 11 (top); © Frederick Florin/AFP/Getty Images, p. 11 (bottom); U.S. Army Photo by C-52 of 3/2 Stryker Brigade Combat Team, p. 12; U.S. Army Photo, p. 13 (top); U.S. Army Photo by Cpl. Oh Chi-hyung, p. 13 (bottom); © Alexis Rosenfeld/Photo Researchers, Inc., p. 14; © imagebroker.net/SuperStock, p. 15 (top); © Dave Darnell/ZUMA Press/CORBIS, p. 15 (bottom); © Doug Pensinger/Getty Images, p. 16; © iStockphoto.com/Vesna Andjic, p. 17 (top); © Ojo Images/Workbook Stock/Getty Images, p. 17 (bottom); © Dave Yoder/Aurora Photos/Alamy, p. 18; © Rob Gallagher/ZUMA Press, p. 19; © Tom Pennington/Getty Images, p. 20; © Jon Feingersh/Iconica/Getty Images, p. 21 (top); © Geoff Burke/Getty Images, p. 21 (bottom); © John Moore/Getty Images, p. 22; U.S. Navy photo by Mass Communication Specialist 2nd Class William S. Parker, p. 23 (top); U.S. Naval Special Warfare, p. 23 (bottom); NASA, pp. 24, 25 (inset); © Roberto Gonzalez/Getty Images, p. 25; © Luc Novovitch/Alamy, p. 26; © iStockphoto.com/Brian Gudas, p. 27 (top); © Robert McGouey/All Canada Photos/Getty Images, p. 27 (bottom); © Saeed Khan/AFP/Getty Images, p. 28; AP Photo/Ivor Prickett, Sunday Times, p. 29.

Front cover: © Aly Song/Reuters/CORBIS.

Main body text set in Calvert MT Std Regular 11/16.
Typeface provided by Monotype Typography.